I'm a little scientist!

I CAN CHANGE THE WORLD...

See a QR code? Scan it to access bonus resources!

WITH THE CHOICE OF MY FOOD

BY
RONALD CHAN  ILLUSTRATED BY
YEEWEARN

WS Education

NEW JERSEY · LONDON · SINGAPORE · BEIJING · SHANGHAI · HONG KONG · TAIPEI · CHENNAI · TOKYO

My passion for good food began at the neighbourhood hawker centre.

As I grew up, I watched and then helped my parents at their food stall, alongside many other stalls that were magically whipping up delicious local dishes.

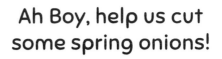

Soon, I started taking pictures of the delicious food that surrounded me day in and day out, and sharing them with others on the Internet. I called myself Mr Food Snapper.

However, as I embarked on my food adventures, I gradually noticed one thing: that people in many places were wasting a lot of food.

After an online search, I found out that possibly a third of all the world's food is either lost or wasted!

For the sake of our future, I knew that this could not continue...

And thus, Mr Food Saver was born!

On weekdays, I was still Mr Food Snapper, sharing photos of our beloved cuisine with others.

FRIDAY

SUNDAY

But on weekends, I became Mr Food Saver, beginning my small crusade against food wastage.

My first stop this weekend is an all-you-can-eat buffet restaurant.
I look around and notice a boy carrying a mountain of food back to his table. I stop to observe him for a while.

Mum, Dad, we're getting our money's worth here!

Oh dear, that's too much! How are we going to finish all this?

Uh oh, they're leaving without finishing their food!
I decide that it's time for me to step in.

Hey, buddy! That's a lot of food you've left behind. Why did you take so much in the first place?

HELP TO
REDUCE
FOOD WASTAGE!
TAKE ONLY WHAT
YOU CAN FINISH.

I wanted to try a little of everything! Besides, there's so much food here that it doesn't matter. This buffet is so cheap!

Well, my friend, every bit matters. By choosing to waste less food, you can change the world!

Hmm… How so? And wait, aren't you Mr Food Snapper? I've seen many of your photos online!

That's right! But today I'm Mr Food Saver. Join me in this video, and we'll find out how the choice of your food matters!

I'll be your guide as we take in the scenery and explore our food story. Let's start at the very beginning, shall we?

Yes, Mr Food Saver!

Our surroundings shift and morph into a farm, and we are now a part of our own food documentary.

"We are at a farm where our food is grown. With the choice of your food, you decide how much needs to be produced."

But Mr Food Saver, how do farms produce methane?

Farms utilise a large amount of natural resources and have considerable environmental impact. Agriculture often drives deforestation and consumes more than half of our fresh water.

"Farms need land and water for crops and livestock. They may even produce methane, which traps heat on Earth! By ordering only the food we need, farms can produce just the right amount, and we can help conserve our resources and cool our planet."

MEET NEWTON,

a cow grazing in the field. Certain farm animals like cattle and sheep produce methane because of the way they digest food, as does rice in certain conditions. As a greenhouse gas like carbon dioxide, methane prevents heat from escaping the planet and is responsible for global warming. By growing only what's needed, farms can help to slow down climate change!

When cows burp and rice fields are flooded!

⚠ While food is essential for our survival and we cannot avoid producing it, we can help conserve these precious resources by taking and consuming only what we need!

"After farms harvest their crops, they need to send them to our supermarkets and eateries using vehicles. Trucks, vans and planes can pollute our air and also warm our planet!"

Farms require vehicles to harvest and transport crops. Many of these vehicles burn fuel in their engines and generate exhaust gases. Soot particles can eventually cause problems with breathing, while other exhaust gases contribute to smog, acid rain and global warming.

Fresh

Cafe

MEET EDISON,

an electric truck that runs on energy stored in batteries! Edison is usually plugged in to charge at night so that it has enough energy for the day. Since it does not directly burn fuel, Edison reduces pollution and slows down climate change – provided the area Edison runs in does not generate electricity by burning fossil fuels like coal or natural gas!

So by not wasting food, we can make fewer of these trips and protect our environment?

That's right!

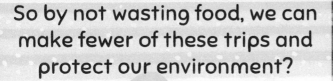

⚠ A lower demand for food creates a cleaner supply chain that is more sustainable for the environment.

"Here we are at a tray return station in a hawker centre."

PAPER   GLASS   PLASTIC   FOOD

Where does all the uneaten food go?

Into the rubbish bin!

Yes. Let's check out what happens to the garbage after it's collected.

! Unfinished food has to be disposed like all other waste. Waste is collected regularly to prevent odours and pests.

The uneaten food is taken to a landfill or burnt in an incinerator. By reducing our food waste, these facilities will pollute our environment less. We could also save space taken up by landfills!

Wow, yes, that's a huge landfill!

MEET VALERIE,

a scientist developing new methods for **food waste valorisation!** This is the process of turning food waste into useful products. Popular examples include the composting of vegetable scraps and coffee grounds into fertilisers for gardens, and the upcycling of fruit peels into seedling pots and kitchen cleaners. Do you have other ideas for food waste valorisation at home?

⚠ Some food waste may be transported to an incinerator to be burnt with other plastic and metal waste, which may generate toxic gases and ash that have to be properly handled. However, some energy may be recoverable from the burning process for other uses. Waste that is not burnt is deposited in a landfill to decompose, generating carbon dioxide and methane, which are not good for our climate! Efforts are underway to capture some of these gases to mitigate their impact.

"Any plate of food that is wasted could be a meal for another family. While we try to reduce food wastage, let's also think about how we can help others around us who may be less well-off."

MEET PARKER,

a volunteer with a local organisation that helps to redistribute excess food to those in need. Parker helps to collect unexpired canned and packaged food donations. He sorts and packs them, then brings them to the homes of the recipients. Can you play a part in your local community as well?

DONATION

While the amount of food waste has steadily increased over the years as the world becomes more affluent, so has the level of food insecurity for those less well-off. To be food-secure, one should have access to enough food every day to remain happy and healthy.

Did you know that we already produce enough food for everyone on the planet, even though about one in three people still do not eat well? Let's make an effort to direct food to everyone who needs it!

I want to be a responsible member of my community and look out for my neighbours!

I snap my fingers and we find ourselves back in the buffet restaurant.

Smaller environmental
impact by farms

Lower pollutant emissions from
farm-to-fork transportation

Wow, thanks, Mr Food Saver, I have learnt a lot from you! One action has many effects. By choosing to waste less food, I can make the world a more sustainable place!

That's right! Let's recap how you can change the world with just the choice of your food.

Less food waste to store or burn

Increased food security for all

"Now, off you go," I tell the boy. "Remember to eat well, stay healthy and take only what you can finish next time!"

"Yes, Mr Food Saver!" he says eagerly. He goes off, hurrying to catch up with his parents.

That's the end of another fulfilling day, I think to myself. But the work does not stop here. Mr Food Saver will continue to do his duty every weekend to encourage others to reduce food wastage!

Be a Food Saver, like Me!

HELP YOUR COMMUNITY!

When families purchase too much food at their local supermarket or grocery store, or when bakeries and delis make too much food for the day, much of this is often prematurely discarded and goes to waste. Community organisations, such as food banks and charities, help to prevent this by collecting and redistributing food while it's still good and wholesome to eat.

Find out more about such organisations in the area where you live, and see if there are any volunteer opportunities available if you're interested to help!

DONATION

Can you think of other sources of food that are often good to eat but are thrown out anyway?

★ Hint: How often have you seen a spotted banana or a bruised apple being sold? What can you do about it?

DID YOU NOTICE?

Did you notice these during Mr Food Saver's adventures? See how you can help to reduce food wastage and its impact.

PORTION SIZE

SMALL	$2.50	serves 1
LARGE	$3.00	serves 1–2
extra meat	extra rice	
$3.00	$0.80	

HELP TO **REDUCE** FOOD WASTAGE: TAKE ONLY WHAT YOU CAN FINISH.

Order only what you can finish (Pg4, 12): If you're not sure how hungry you are, start with less food on your plate! You can always order or take more food later. If you're new to the eatery, you can also ask for advice on food portions.

Sort your food waste (Pg20): If your local eatery or waste collection point has a separate bin for food waste, please use it! This helps food waste to be treated and upcycled more effectively.

Are there other ways to reduce food wastage and its impact?

Look out for these as well! Here are other ways to lead a sustainable lifestyle.

Reusable food containers (Pg2, 4): Excessive use of single-use takeaway containers contributes significantly to our waste problem. If you're ordering food to take back to your home or office, bring along your own reusable food container instead!

Transportation (Pg19): When we commute from one place to another, the choice of our transportation contributes differently to greenhouse gas emissions. Whenever possible, use public transport such as buses or trains instead of private transport.

WHAT CAN I DO AT HOME?

Do you or your family cook at home? Here are more ways to reduce food wastage:

Use the freezer: If you have leftovers, not to worry! Pack them into portions and freeze them, and they'll still be good when reheated for the next meal or two.

Buy only what you need: Encourage your family to plan meals ahead of time, and buy only what's necessary during your groceries trip, keeping in mind what you already have at home.

Share your food: Share the delicacies you prepared with your friends and neighbours. This will prevent your excess food from going to waste, and also build neighbourly ties and friendships!

Could you try growing your own food or making your own fertiliser?

HOW CAN I GET OTHERS TO JOIN IN?

Here's how you can encourage those around you to learn more about food wastage and how to reduce it:

Organise a Clean Plate challenge in your school's canteen:
Rope in your classmates and teachers for a Clean Plate challenge to encourage them not to waste food! Food trays should be returned after meals without any leftovers.

(Talk to your canteen's stall owners or food providers to accommodate requests for different food portions, so that people do not force themselves to finish excess food!)

Look out for local enrichment activities and volunteer opportunities:
Encourage your friends and family to join you in visits to your local waste management facility or food bank, and learn more about waste management and food redistribution together.

Join a club or write in:
Look out for clubs or societies in your school relating to zero-waste practices or sustainability, or create one on your own if it doesn't exist! Help to spread awareness of the issue by organising activities and writing to your school's magazine or local newspaper.

 What are other ways to help and to spread the word?

Published by
WS Education, an imprint of
World Scientific Publishing Co. Pte. Ltd.
5 Toh Tuck Link, Singapore 596224
USA office: 27 Warren Street, Suite 401–402, Hackensack, NJ 07601
UK office: 57 Shelton Street, Covent Garden, London WC2H 9HE

National Library Board, Singapore Cataloguing in Publication Data
Name(s): Chan, Ronald, author. | Yee Wearn, illustrator.
Title: I can change the world ... with the choice of my food / written by Ronald Chan ; illustrated by Yeewearn.
Other Title(s): I'm a scientist! (WS Education (Firm))
Description: Singapore : WS Education, [2022]
Identifier(s): ISBN 978-981-12-5751-3 (hardback) | 978-981-12-5752-0 (paperback) |
    978-981-12-5753-7 (ebook for institutions) | 978-981-12-5754-4 (ebook for individuals)
Subject(s): LCSH: Food waste--Juvenile fiction. | Sustainable living--Juvenile fiction.
Classification: DDC 428.6--dc23

British Library Cataloguing–in–Publication Data
A catalogue record for this book is available from the British Library.

For any available supplementary material, please visit
https://www.worldscientific.com/worldscibooks/10.1142/12880#t=suppl

Printed in Singapore